To Daddy

From Alistair

Christmas 1986

lots of love + best wishes

FRANCOME
IN PICTURES

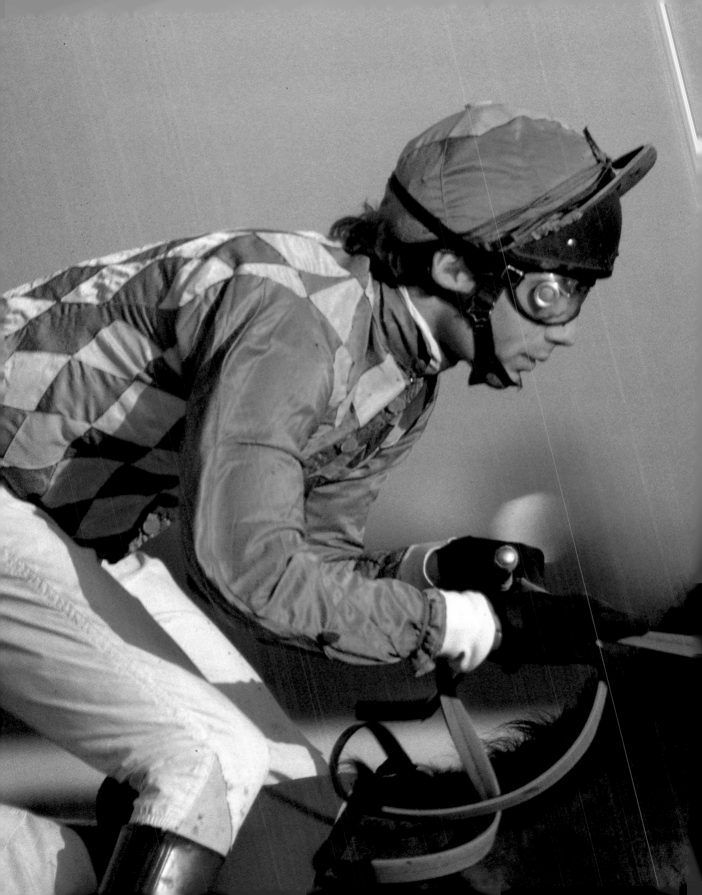

FRANCOME
IN PICTURES

CAPTIONS BY JOHN FRANCOME

PARTRIDGE PRESS

Published in Great Britain by
Partridge Press
Maxwelton House
Boltro Road
Haywards Heath
West Sussex

Partridge Press is an imprint of Transworld Publishers Limited
61/63 Uxbridge Road
London W5 5SA

Designed by Graeme Murdoch

Reproduced and proofed by Adroit Photo Litho Limited, Birmingham.

Phototypeset by Tradespools Limited, Frome
Printed and bound in Great Britain by
W.S. Cowell Limited, Ipswich.

ISBN 1-85225-015 1

It's muddy lovely. Another record under the belt – the fastest 50 in a season recorded at Cheltenham on 11 November 1984. The second 50 that season took a great deal longer.

INTRODUCTION

BY RICHARD PITMAN

Jump jockeys are a rare breed of men and John Francome was certainly one of the rarest. Having worked with him since he left school I would describe him as a controlled extrovert, with a ready wit and a natural magnetism.

Just like Fred Winter, his only employer, the curly haired cavalier would certainly have emerged at the top of some other heap had racing not been invented. Unlike many of his colleagues, who have to be forced out of the game due to injury or diminishing support, John made his exit while his fans were still hungry for more of his artistry in the saddle.

Then, as indeed throughout his life, the Wiltshire man listened to 'the vibes' that so many only acknowledge in hindsight. When lying in the Chepstow grass with The Reject using John as a foot stool, it occurred to the winning-most jockey of all time 'that fifty quid less expenses per ride was perhaps after all not a particularly good deal'. Just weeks earlier the same horse had warned his pilot that not all falls result in the rider flying through the air with the greatest of ease. At Cheltenham John experienced every rider's dread when hanging upside-down trapped by a stirrup leather; never a slow thinker, he grabbed The Reject's reins while still dangling, forcing the excited chaser to circle instead of galloping after disappearing rivals. Had that not happened serious if not fatal injury would have been the result. To this day John has not lost his nerve, as even a short car ride with him will prove, but The Reject's fall did confirm that 'life has so many other things to offer'.

Fifteen years earlier the aspiring jockey walked into his first and only job as 'one of the bunch' at Fred Winter's Lambourn stables. Being the retained jockey I viewed each of the new jockeys as potential dangers. Franc's body told me he would be lucky to stay light enough to be a serious threat, although his personality and obvious talent as a horseman allerted my sixth sense.

He had missed the days when we lived in a collection of old caravans and the only way to squirm out of emptying the portable loos was to pay someone else to take the shift. When John arrived a new hostel housed the lads, but even this was a shock to his system at first.

Having been brought up at Swindon in relative luxury by parents who spoiled him with love, it was quite an adjustment to wake up to the odour of stiff socks and compressed horse muck in wellington boots. Even so it took no time at all for the young Francome to realise that to get on he had to be one of the lads, while at the same time be better than them.

'Yes' men's action may curry favour for a while then eventually the music has to be faced. It is a definite way to go one step forward though surely in time the 'yes' man jumps two paces back. John's plan of attack was quite different. It was firstly to do his job properly, then to make himself useful to those who were able to help him on his way. Baby-sitting for Head Lad Brian Delaney and myself killed two birds with one stone. Instead of spending money in the evenings, he was earning some, plus chalking up a few favours to be used in the future.

Replacing window panes, doing carpentry repairs, plugging holes in the roof or making obstinate motors surge into life, were just a few of the odd jobs that came easy to him, but John was never an odd bod. Again the reasoning behind these moves was two-fold, "I hated doing horses during evening stables and it occurred to me that jockeys got paid for riding, not grooming".

On the Berkshire Downs the newcomer stood out for diverse reasons. He was big compared to other youngsters which made him look rather ungainly. "Agricultural" was the description that sticks in my mind. That plus the size of his hands and feet combined to appear as if John Francome's days in racing would be numbered, yet then as today when his back is against the wall Francome's brain works best.

He reasoned that winning jump races must be allied to the economy of energy over the obstacles and jumping was his strongest point. Schooling sessions are touchy times even when things go right, but that changed when John arrived. Debutantes relaxed for him, nervous horses found bravery from somewhere, hard pullers settled, bad jumpers made fewer mistakes. Most important as John's role increased, these sessions became fun and believe me that is unusual.

John's showjumping experience put him literally years ahead of other school leavers entering stables, and had also educated him to deal with people. If it took a little persuasion for my outside contacts to support him initially, a second engagement was John's for the asking. Even so he displayed a sense of fair play which was a hallmark few people knew of. Never once did he try to keep either mine or other jockeys' regular rides. Spares were fair game, but bread and butter jobs were sacrosanct.

As John established himself, his business eye opened wide. When securing a mount for one of the other young jockeys he would charge them £2 commission. It made sense; without his contacts the others would certainly not have got the work, and were well pleased with the deal. Come to think of it he was probably the first jockey's agent in Britain!

Never backward in coming forward he set his sights on marrying well right from an early age – love did not figure in the calculation! He had no difficulty dating well bred fillies and seldom took the same girl out twice in a row. "She'd got elder brothers" was the usual reason. Not, I hasten to add, because he had an aversion to males, but it naturally affected the beauty's inheritance.

Even the best laid plans go astray and sure enough Cupid found John an easier target than he had envisaged. After his third date with Miriam Strigner we all assumed John had found his only child heiress. "It's crazy, she's the youngest of six children, but I get this strange tingle when we're together, I've never felt it before" was his report.

The romance blossomed and reached fruition ten years ago when this ideal pair married in London. When we were waiting for Miriam to join us at the altar, John had a far-away look prompting me to say "What's on your mind John? If you're not sure she's the right girl now's the time to pull out, not afterwards". Typical of the man he replied "Miriam's definitely the girl for me, I was just wondering how much the priest would take for those tiles around the side of the altar!"

Today the couple represent as strong a union as imaginable, and are really good friends. If anything, now training, it has given Miriam a closer relationship with her husband. As a jockey she could only be an observer, along with the other racegoers. Of course she was always there to pick up the pieces after a crashing fall, but race-riding is a one man operation, it can be lonely. Now, riding out with the string, even leading the babies over jumps on her hack Snowtown Boy, and dealing with the horse-owners, gives Miriam the rewarding sense of being useful. As a pair they complement each other to make a strong team.

Snowtown Boy was in fact one of the horses John used to display his cheek, even under the pressure of racing. At Newbury the pair drew alongside Bob Champion two fences from home without having used the obvious overdrive Snowtown Boy possessed. Instead of giving in, to record a facile victory, John kept Bob company, forcing his colleague to work overtime. Even from the grandstand it was obvious John was playing Champion as if he were a salmon. It was only in the last few strides the seven times champion gave Snowy his head and ceased his verbal taunts. Snowtown Boy returned to the winner's enclosure fresh as paint, whereas Champs knew he'd been in a fight.

If that was cheeky, John's handling of Sea Pigeon in the Champion Hurdle was artistry to the limit. He nursed the enigmatic character on the heels of the leaders, sitting motionless. Even after the last hurdle, when every nerve must have been screaming messages to his brain to kick on, he kidded Sea Pigeon it was a morning gallop not hurdling's crown that was at stake.

For his timing and deliverance the jester came out top. John had always been known as a brilliant horseman which implied he was not a jockey. This victory stamped him as both.

Strangely John brushed aside praise for his riding talent, yet he did rate people who thought enough of him as a human being to enquire after his injuries after the inevitable fall. It is generally accepted that the average jump jockey will walk back (if he's lucky) one in every ten occasions he starts a race. Franc halved that ratio by sheer command of the situation. Even so he made some of his own luck. Always one to walk the course before racing, if conditions had changed through weather or movable running rails, he surprised me at Newbury on a seemingly normal day.

As I followed John's lone walk through my binoculars it was plain to see his mission. At each flight of hurdles the rider stopped, took hold of the outside-but-one section and manoeuvred it back and forth until it was loose. Having considerably reduced the strength of the obstacle John then covered his tracks by re-aligning his section with the rest of the flight supported with a small stick. Hiding his work was just as important as doing it, because a dilligent groundsman would have assuredly hammered any apparently sloppy sections back into shape, defeating the object of the exercise for John.

Keen to confirm my evaluation I met the mischievous man when he came back off the course. "Mine in the 3-year-old hurdle is a head-strong sod and he'll be fighting me, not looking where he's going over the first four hurdles. If I can't waggon him from the saddle I thought it wise to alter the odds of survival – his and mine!" The ruse worked as far as getting to the finish intact was concerned, although nothing the champion

No, it's not Royal Ascot. Best man Richard Pitman and John nervously await the main event of the day outside the Roman Catholic Church in Spanish Place, London, on 26 June 1976.

did could persuade the horse to gallop faster than his rivals.

Right to the end of his incredible riding career, John never gave up his quest to do better. Even winning rides were dissected on video tape to see if any aspects of his performance could be improved. Aspiring Francomes should take note. The action photos in this book alone will help riders to improve their liaison between horse and jump. The most obvious difference between John and lesser lights is shown clearly by his position prior to take off. Having judged the horse's stride pattern sufficiently well to meet a fence without recourse to sudden correction, John noticeably lowers his body into the horse, almost becoming a part of it. Many others, including some of the better-known jockeys, set their horses up well then reverse the Francome take-off position by sitting upright.

Horses can be put off by riders just as easily as they can be aided, and John's instructions to his equine partners were hardly visible and almost always listened to. Horses with half a brain could not fail to respond to the confidence they received from him via hands and lower legs. Through the reins to their mouth then to the brain, from the grip by his legs through their ribs to the heart then to the brain, commands were given to put horses on alert or at their ease.

Although Grand National victory evaded him, Francome's skill was never more evident than around those huge tricky fences. Rough and Tumble finished third, and then second in that race, yet without John's expertise I do not think the gelding would have got as near as he did. He saved so much valuable energy by precision jumping that

Life begins as a trainer. Tommy Stack, former champion jump jockey and now a top blood stock agent, gives me a few pointers at Newmarket Sales.

the Minister of Energy himself would have been proud of John. Furthermore he went so tight to the inside running rail (where the brave men go) that he took the paint off it. Ironically the same horse had no qualms about depositing his rider in the water at the famous Becher's Brook at the third attempt at the race.

Few people apart from the horse's connections will ever realise that one of John's proudest moments is buried in the 'also ran' from the 1981 Grand National. Riding the ex-Irish chaser So, John had confided in me his honest opinion of his chances. "We are millions against, and that is just to complete" were his words. "He's just too clumsy to get away with it 30 times". Apart from the water jump the other 29 obstacles were negotiated with relative safety, as a result of the rider's actions. He anchored So with such determination that the horse thought he was in a dentist's chair, not the races. Using the *puissance* technique, he made every fence the big wall at Wembley, never once giving So the benefit of the doubt. It was indeed a personal victory for Francome to complete the course, and a major disaster for me as I had specifically knocked him out of my list of four to complete the course.

If jockeys are renowned for being bad tipsters I can only assure you it is based on bitter experience. After John's much publicised battle and following his association with John Banks he staunchly defended his rights to continue telling the Lambourn tradesmen if he had fancied rides. I admired his forthrightness, but felt sorry for the butcher and the milkman.

Like many people who profess not to be sentimental towards horses the truth is likely to be the opposite. When Lanzarote, Bula and Childown had to be destroyed Franc was as upset as the next man if not more so.

Undoubtedly his own man, John is nevertheless a definite mixture of his parents' qualities and idiosyncrasies. Quite rightly he has always been aware that in the end everybody crumbles, which has meant that John Francome is what he is. Pretence is not in his dictionary, he is a good friend to those he likes and ignores the others without bearing malice.

These photographs will give you a good indication of John Francome the jockey and the man, although his most personal side is well disguised. Despite a hectic life, he drives long distances to visit hospitalised colleagues, even years after the game has passed them by and the more obscure have been forgotten. Now as he settles into the second half of his working life John Francome's name is likely to be less in evidence, though somehow I doubt it.

RICHARD PITMAN
August, 1986

11

Here I am in my role as a deep-lying centre-forward. Twin sisters Jill (left)
and Norma are on the wing. A glance at my girth even at this early stage
suggests there was never any threat of me becoming a Flat jockey.
I had a good seat even at the age of two. I'm not sure we had any
armchairs in those days! The reluctant family photo features Dad, Mum,
the twins, me and one of my first four-legged friends.

Keep them coming! Receiving a rosette for my first
venture on the bigger ponies. This one is Raindrop,
owned by friend and neighbour John Whiteman. The gong
was for winning the musical poles at Highworth, near Swindon.

Richard Branson, eat your heart out! That's me doing a
tidying up job at a local show near Swindon. I'm riding
Willie Wagtail, a complete freak but still the prettiest
pony I have ever seen. He had wall-to-wall grey spots!

Red Paul carries me safely off the
side of the Derby Bank at
Hickstead in 1969. Without this
horse I would probably have lost
interest in riding altogether. Just
12 months later he won the
Hickstead Young Riders
Championship for me.

An early fashion shot from 1972. You needed short hair in those days if you wanted to get on.

Multigrey, giving me a win on my first ride in public at Worcester on 2 December 1970. Thankfully there is no picture of my second ride. I fell and broke a wrist.

Above, Osbaldeston, the race horse to whom I owe everything. I'd had my fill of stable work and was getting nowhere as a jockey until I was introduced to this character. I was given a ride on him at Worcester and his 1½ length victory provided the encouragement I needed.

Left, an early ride for Ken Cundell, one of the many 'outside' trainers to whom my mate Richard Pitman recommended me.

Here I am in second place on Sonny Somers at Stratford in 1973. I am in pursuit of David Mould, my boyhood hero and the man on whom I modelled myself. When I had won on my first ride, it was David who observed: 'You looked bloody awful.'

Men's fashion (background) at my Lambourn yard, circa 1975. These are not the clothes I wore to build the stable.

Left, the 'red shack', where I lived while I was building my home and stables in Lambourn. My wife Miriam watches as I wait patiently for Bruin the dobermann to clean up his act before letting him into the family runabout.

Just four of the many faces of my old guv'nor Fred Winter. The younger generation of race fans may not realise just what a great jockey they missed seeing. He was champion four times and won every big race going – that's him being led in on Eborneezer after landing the 1961 Champion Hurdle at Cheltenham. He also won two Gold Cups and two Grand Nationals.

Despite success in the saddle he proved an even better trainer. Eight times champion, he is seen receiving the latest (hopefully, not the last) of his awards at the William Hill Golden Spurs lunch in the London Hilton in February 1986. He can be a demon when roused – especially first thing on a cold winter's morning – but he also owns a keen sense of humour as you can appreciate from the picture of him letting his hair down at my retirement party on Newbury racecourse.

Former Champion Hurdler Lanza-rote (right) took well to chasing and looked as though he could go to the very top. But Fred Winter's count-less moments of glory have always been punctuated by disaster. Lanza-rote broke a leg in the 1977 Gold Cup and was destroyed.

My one and only Cheltenham Gold Cup. Midnight Court does the business in the race, owner Olive Jackson enjoys her proud moment afterwards and, with hand signals, I explain to guv'nor Fred Winter just how easy it all was.

Some you win, some you lose. Rough and Tumble giving me a great ride to finish third in the 1979 Grand National (above) and the same horse looking at his handiwork after taking a dislike to jumping Becher's Brook for a second time in the 1982 race. I wish I had known what was in his mind – I could have saved myself an uncomfortable moment and a hefty laundry bill!

One Armed Bandit on his way to victory in a
novice chase at the big post-Christmas
Kempton meeting in 1982. Colin Brown had
shown the good sense to get off No 17 at an
earlier fence.

I was beaten on more favourites in the Daily
Express Triumph Hurdle than Tetley have tea
bags. This is Rodman at Cheltenham in 1978
about to add to the record.

Lucky for some 13. This is So cooling himself off in the water at Liverpool in 1981. Twenty-nine of the fences there are enormous but So decides to make his big mistake at the only other one.

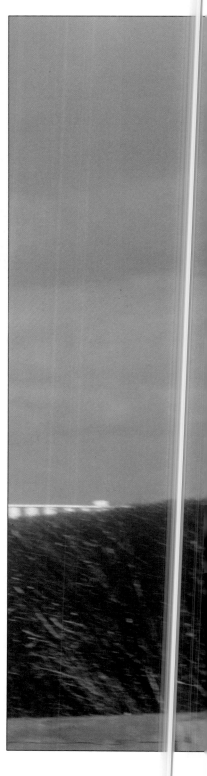

Teaming up with the great Grittar (above). Unfortunately, he never liked me quite as much as he did that brilliant amateur Dick Saunders, who steered him to a remarkable victory in the 1982 Grand National.

Right, Observe measures a fence at Newbury.

Right, they don't come much tougher than this. It's Paul Kelleway's Donegal Prince, a winner on the Flat, over hurdles and in chases. My big moment on him came in the 1982 Schweppes Gold Trophy at Newbury. I put up 4 lb overweight but luckily we won by a head. Otherwise 'Kelloggs' might have had something to say.

One of the last big winners I rode. Above, Wayward Lad, perhaps the best horse never to win the Cheltenham Gold Cup, captures the Whitbread Gold Label Chase at Liverpool in March 1985.

The 12-nation line-up for the first Railfreight National Hunt Jockeys World Championship in 1984. Happily, I won it despite pulling up on the last of my rides. The star turn, however, was Shinobu Hoshimo, the little Japanese guy in the middle. He needed so much lead in his saddle he could hardly carry it back to the weighing room.

Steve Smith Eccles and I working hard to prepare for a new season. These pictures from Portugal show that Steve is equally adept with his feet or his hands in water. Left, Andy Turnell and I keep taking the Pils at a charity function.

All pals together before the fray. Tommy Carmody
and myself leaving the Newbury weighing room for
what could not possibly have been a novice chase – we
look too cheerful.

Now this is what I call an award. A mud-spattered
Jonjo O'Neill presents me with a cheque from State
Express at the Cheltenham Festival in March 1979.

A cartoon in the French racing daily *Paris Turf* points to my aerial superiority over my Gallic colleagues. In fact it was my weight, rather than height, that restricted French sorties. Even so, I had my moments . . . here I am on my way to victory on a spare ride at Auteuil.

Young Lover in action at Sandown in January 1983. We lost this one but there were plenty of wins for both he and one of my favourite owners, Mrs Olive Jackson.

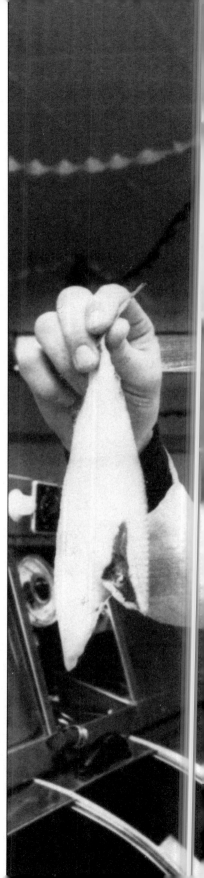

No awards for my prowess as a fish fryer.
But here I am doing my level best in the
Swindon shop I part-own with ex-jockey
Bill Shoemark.

One down, two to go. This is Sea Pigeon, the greatest horse I ever rode, going past Starfen after the last flight in the 1981 Champion Hurdle. Still ahead were Pollardstown and Daring Run. We beat them too and Sea Pigeon earned the congratulations of an adoring public.

The lissom youth seen diving into the pool is me attempting to regain fitness after a bone graft in 1970.

That's me on the far side aboard Grey
Mate for Peter Haynes in the Dick Francis
Novice Chase at Lingfield in December
1983. As with all Dick Francis stories, there
was a sting in the tail. I finished second to
Don't Shout but objected to Richard Rowe
and was awarded the race. The stewards
were kind to me on occasions!

Pride before a fall. Here I am leading on
Glyde Court in a Philip Cornes qualifier at
Ascot in January 1984. Seconds later I was
wiping Berkshire mud off my silks.

Off duty, I will try my hand at any sport,
whether it's trotting in Stockholm, playing
tennis at Honiton or motor racing at
Thruxton.

Something else for Miriam to dust. I was lucky enough
to pick up a number of awards in my riding career but
this one meant more than most. The trophy not only
marked the first World Jump Jockey's Championship, it
was fashioned by my long time friend Philip Blacker,
once a great jockey and now one of our foremost
sculptors.
Taking the strain in the BBC's Superstars contest. Either
it's very heavy or there is a bloke hanging on to each end.
The result? I finished a highly creditable second last,
with Ian Botham one place behind.

On a happier note, Observe lifts me to my
1,000th winner on 29 February 1984. It
was a welcome return to Worcester, the
scene of my very first winner on Multigrey all those years earlier.

Park Rainbow on his way to victory at Newbury in March 1984. The win made it 100 in a season for me for four times. Left, a shot of Nugent in action on the run-in at Sandown in March 1984. It looks impressive but there was a horse out of camera on the right.

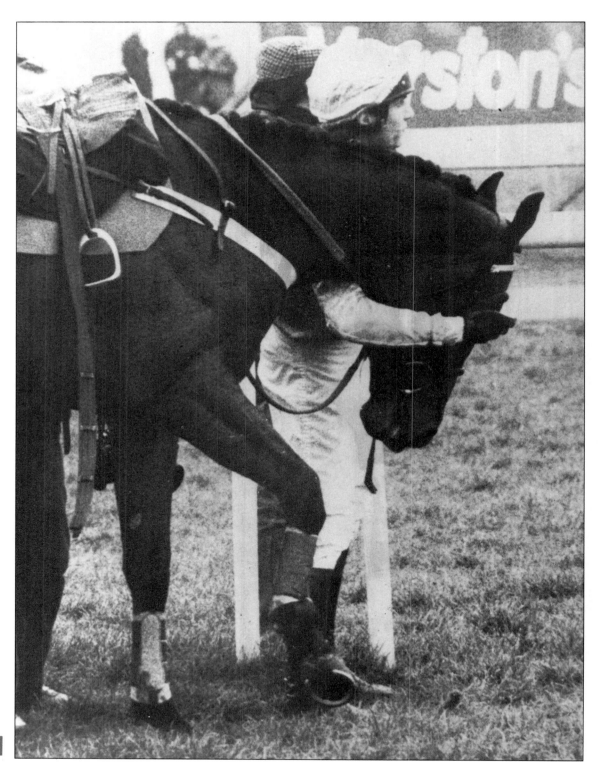

Left, one of the more sad moments of my racing life. Childown breaks a leg after negotiating only two flights in the 1984 Daily Express Triumph Hurdle . . . and pays the ultimate price. Above, another one bites the dust. Hopstone chooses a sparsely attended Newbury fixture in March 1982 to show off his range of circus tricks. My own acrobatics went down well too – except with punters who had backed me.

Up, up and away. Areus carries me
easily enough over the water at
Newbury in March 1984. Unfortunately the next time we were in front
of the stands the others were up, up
and away. I finished last.

Hywel Davies helps
Green Bramble look
for his contact lenses
during the Thunder
and Lightning Chase
at Ascot in January
1984. That was the
end of their race but
I managed to take
evasive action and
finish third on
Carved Opal.

One of the great weight-carrying performances since the days of Arkle.
Burrough Hill Lad makes it look so easy under the crushing burden of 12
stones to win the Hennessy Cognac Gold Cup at Newbury in 1984.

Peter Scudamore (foreground) and I do battle at Kempton in December 1984. The picture flatters me: Peter eventually won on Gainsay; I came third on Gratification.

Brown Chamberlin skips over Newbury's water jump on his way to victory against Wayward Lad in the Compton Chase in February 1984. A month later he ran the race of his life, finishing second in the Tote Cheltenham Gold Cup to Burrough Hill Lad. He was a great servant to a lovely owner – Mrs Coral Samuel.

Win No 1,036 and at last I
have beaten Stan Mellor's all-
time record. The venue is
Fontwell on 28 May 1984; the
horse is Don't Touch. Leading
him in is owner Bob Short.
That's winning trainer John
Jenkins' dad immediately to the
left of the horse.

Hazy Sunset, one of Fred Winter's Irish imports, never quite fulfilled his potential. But he had his 'on' days such as this at Ascot in 1984.

A dicky bird to go with the dicky bows. Captain Miles Gosling, chairman of the Cheltenham
Steeplechasing Company, presents me with a china bird and a framed, signed photograph of
one of my successes on the course.

Right, the proud recipient of an MBE, pictured outside Buckingham Palace.

Pleased to be able to walk away. The Reject caused me grief at Cheltenham 1985 and cost me the winning ride in the Champion Hurdle on See You Then. A couple of weeks later he gets me all strung up at Chepstow. And that's it as far as I am concerned. The end of a promising career...

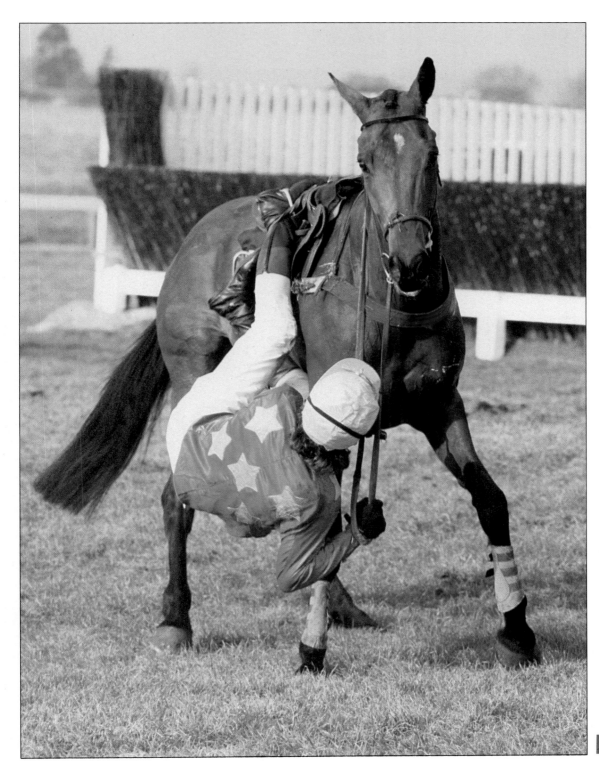

Life as a trainer. Here I am saddling the first winner in my new role – That's Your Lot at Sandown in December 1985. He won at 25–1 and I didn't have a penny on. I had backed him on his previous run at Kempton on the strength of his showing in my own indoor school.

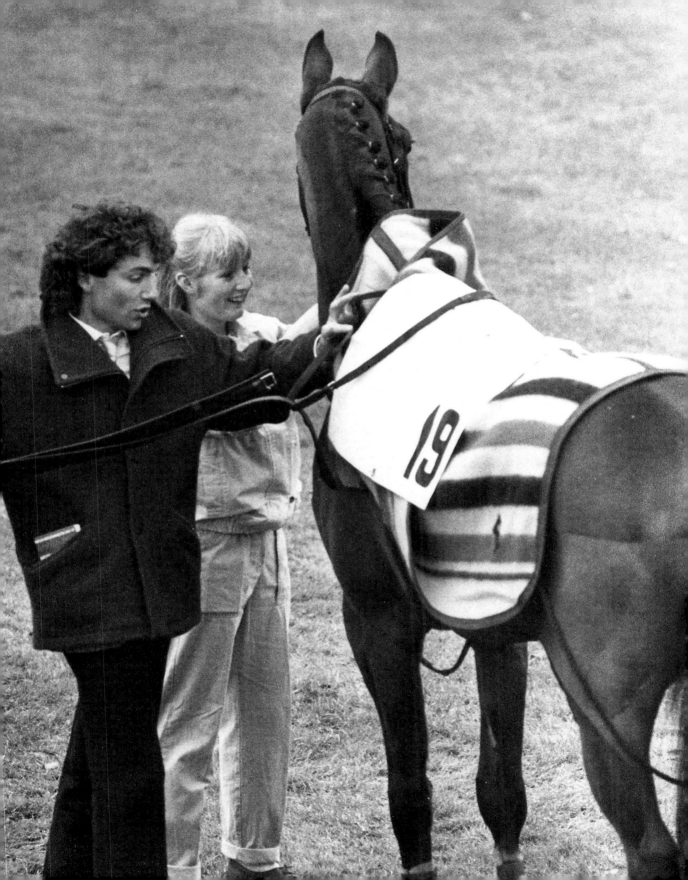

Behind every successful man is a good woman (according to Miriam). That jumping scene is not nearly so hairy as it appears – we were rehearsing for one of those 'lotta bottle' milk adverts. Miriam made her debut as a TV pundit at Royal Ascot in June 1986 and is seen here in a beauty and the beast pose with the BBC's Julian Wilson. Back home Miriam nurses her pet chicken Hazel much to the chagrin of Bruin.

Wing And A Prayer! It's the story of my racing life as trainer John Jenkins supervises me unsaddling Wing And A Prayer after scoring at Sandown in January 1985 – one of five races the horse won that winter. Needless to say, when he started favourite for the Daily Express Triumph Hurdle at the Cheltenham Festival, my jinx held.

Sea Image, probably my favourite horse, making the most of the softer fences at Fontwell.

FRANCOME FACTS

1952	Born 13 December
1969	Signed up for Fred Winter 16 October
1970	Rode first winner on Multigrey at Worcester 2 December
1971	Finished the 70–71 season with four wins from 14 rides
1972	Upped his seasonal tally to 19 wins from 81 rides
1973	Twenty One wins from 128 rides
1974	Thirty wins from 157 rides
1975	Retained as first jockey to Fred Winter.
	Seventy wins from 333 rides put him second in the jockeys' table.
1976	Champion jockey for the first time with 96 wins (392)
	Married Miriam in London 26 June
1977	Second in the title race with 88 wins (373)
1978	Second again – 83 (333)
	Won Cheltenham Gold Cup on Midnight Court
1979	A second championship – 95 (403)
	Third in the Grand National on Rough and Tumble
1980	Second in the Grand National – again on Rough and Tumble
	Only fourth in the championship league – 69 wins (345)
1981	Won the Champion Hurdle on Sea Pigeon
	Regained jockey's title with 105 wins (564)

1982	Joint-champion with Peter Scudamore – 120 wins (549)
	Won Schweppes Gold Trophy on Donegal Prince
	Won King George VI Chase on Wayward Lad
1983	Outright champion – 106 (487)
	Won Hennessy Cognac Gold Cup on Brown Chamberlin and Coral Welsh National on Burrough Hill Lad
1984	Champion with 131 wins (529)
	Won Hennessy Cognac Gold Cup and King George VI on Burrough Hill Lad
1985	Champion jockey for seventh and last time – 101 wins from 373
	Last ride The Reject (fell) at Chepstow 9 April
	First runner as a trainer Crimson Knight at Nottingham 9 September (finished 14th of 20)
	First runner over jumps Crimson Knight at Worcester 14 September (fell when leading, later collapsed and died)
	First winner as a trainer That's Your Lot at Sandown 30 November

Career total of rides: 1,138 wins from 5,061 rides. Champion jockey seven times, three times runner-up in 15 seasons.

Photographic Credits: Gerry and Mark Cranham – 2, 5, 10, 19, 20, 24 (Top), 25, 29, 30, 32, 34, 39, 46, 51, 58, 59, 62, 67, 70, 72, 74, 76, 78, 81, 88, 93, 95. All-Sport – 6, 27 (Top), 38, 66, 83; Wiltshire Newspapers – 14, 15 Findlay Davidson – 18. Sport and General – 26, 31, 36, 55. The Photo Source – 27 (Bottom). London Express News and Features – 33, 53, 60, 65, 68. Sporting Pictures UK – 40, 54, 63, 69, 90. Rex Coleman – 41. Bernard Parkin – 43. R. Simon – 48. Syndication International – 61 (Top), 94. Eimar Anderssons – 61 (Bottom). Pat Larkin – 64. Kenneth Sandalls – 84. Press Association – 85. Colorsport – 86, 87. News of the World – 92.